What Do You Do with an Ousted Liberal?

by
Merrill Matthews, Jr., Ph.D.

Illustrated by Don Adair

Huntington House Publishers
P.O. Box 53788
Lafayette, Louisiana 70505

Library of Congress Card
Catalog Number
95-80936
ISBN 1-56384-112-6

Printed in the U.S.A.

Dedication

To Bill and Hillary Clinton,
without whom
this book would not have
been possible.

Foreword

The elections of 1994 produced wonderful victories for conservatives, but they also dumped thousands of spent humans onto the streets. These lonely souls, known as liberals, hang out everywhere—in television studios, fern bars, and even Jimmy Carter book signings. Their constant presence mocks us by reminding us that the most advanced civilization in history still can't find any constructive use for such people.

Merrill Matthews solves the problem with this important book, while proving once and for all that conservatives have bottomless compassion for the wretched of the earth. Open any page, and you will find a suggestion that could save a lost life, accompanied by a cool cartoon.

Americans have always tempered their revolutions with a little tenderness. Matthews' volume offers dozens of suggestions for helping politically challenged leftists play constructive roles in the "Newt" World Order. If you care about your fellow humans, read this book. Pass it on. And remember: With a little love, guidance and encouragement, liberals can become people, too.

—Tony Snow,
Detroit News and
USA Today

"Backword"

Liberals believe that the conservative landslide in the 8 November 1994 elections resulted in a huge step backward for America. Conservatives may agree with that assessment, but think that is precisely the direction we should be going:

BACK, to a time when the Constitution meant what it said;

BACK, to a time when the Tenth Amendment was as important as the First Amendment;

BACK, to a time when moral values and religion were seen as the foundation of American society, not the destroyer;

BACK, to a time when Congress was limited and Americans were free, not the other way around;

BACK, to a time when politicians understood that Americans don't like taxation, even with representation.

Because this book looks nostalgically backward, it only seems appropriate to include a word about that past—hence, "Backword."

So, what *do* you do with an ousted liberal?

Mount and hang as trophies in
Newt Gingrich's office.

Attach to helium balloons and let them cover the hole in the ozone layer.

Permit to figure out ways to counter the influence of Rush Limbaugh.

Donate to the Washington Zoo so that future generations can marvel at such maladaptive creatures.

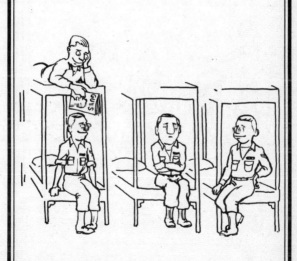

Assign to bunks closest to the gays in the military.

Enroll in midnight basketball programs to keep them off our streets and out of mischief.

Allow to sneak across the border to Mexico, where liberal politicians can still find work.

• Deport from the U.S. to a Third World country and raise the IQs of both countries.

• Include them under the Endangered Species Act, thus ensuring their extinction.

• Nominate to the board of directors of the American Civil Liberties Union.

• Label as lobbyists, freeing them to be open about working for whoever offers the largest paycheck.

Require to seek out surgeon general nominees even more controversial than Drs. Joycelyn Elders and Henry Foster.

License as barbers so they can cut Bill's hair for two hundred bucks a pop.

Offer steady work on the "David Letterman Show" doing "stupid liberal tricks."

Add a few more to the economics faculty at Harvard.

Donate their brains to medical science so researchers can study frontal lobe abnormalities.

RASTENKOWSKI

Allow to evolve to a higher life form.

Provide hot air to float balloons in Macy's Thanksgiving Day Parade.

Audition a few for their favorite role: Robin Hood.

Transport to New Orleans to write and sing the blues.

Assign to the endless task of explaining the defeat of the Clinton health care plan.

• Encourage the formation of a 1996 presidential exploratory committee called "Give Gore Four."

• Make attending Newt Gingrich's "Renewing American Civilization" course a requirement.

• Give each of them one thousand dollars to do "amateur" investing in cattle futures.

• Encourage to seek grants from the National Endowment for the Arts for offensive art with no redeeming value.

Force each to repair the many chips they created in America's moral foundation.

Enlist as U.N. Peacekeepers—
assigned to the First Family.

Position as targets on NRA firing ranges.

Dispatch to Cuba to enjoy the benefits of living in a "worker's paradise."

Have them work to pass term limits, since that may be their only hope of getting conservatives out of office.

Advance the Keep America Beautiful program by depositing them in roadside cans.

Use as paperweights for all the
Republican bills passing the House.

Use as substitute anchors when Dan Rather and Tom Brokaw go on vacation.

Employ at the IRS where they can confiscate taxpayer money directly, rather than through the legislative process.

Volunteer for a David Copperfield show—in which he makes them all disappear.

Hire for commercials for large, capitalistic companies such as Frito-Lay.

• Sign on as political pollsters where they can ensure that future polls will prove that Americans agree with what liberals think.

• Send as U.S. ambassadors to other countries, which will at least get them out of this country.

• Allow their intellectual handicap to be protected under the Americans with Disabilities Act.

• Train as counselors offering job placement advice to future ousted liberals.

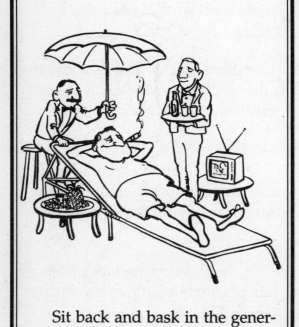

Sit back and bask in the generous, taxpayer funded, retirement plans they voted for themselves.

Create a virtual reality program in which liberals could actually win an election.

Mount as weather vanes to point out which direction the political wind is blowing.

Hire as department store Santa Clauses in recognition of their ability to make promises and hand out goodies.

• Establish a Spendaholics Anonymous center, where they can be treated for their addiction to spending other people's money.

• Retrain as many as possible to do an honest day's work.

• Take teaching positions in public schools arranged for by the National Education Association.

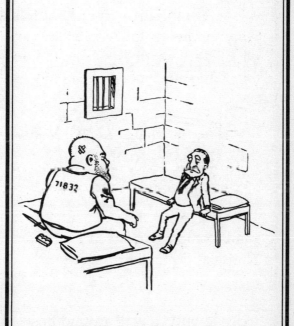

Assign to share the cells of death row "victims."

Use to build a wall around Boston in order to keep future generations of liberals from escaping.

Convert to conservatives so they can win reelection next time.

ALSO AVAILABLE FROM HUNTINGTON HOUSE